Spooky Spots

SPOOKY HOSPITALS

JESSICA RUSICK

Big Buddy Books

An Imprint of Abdo Publishing
abdobooks.com

abdobooks.com

Published by Abdo Publishing, a division of ABDO, PO Box 398166, Minneapolis, Minnesota 55439. Copyright © 2021 by Abdo Consulting Group, Inc. International copyrights reserved in all countries. No part of this book may be reproduced in any form without written permission from the publisher. Big Buddy Books™ is a trademark and logo of Abdo Publishing.

Printed in the United States of America, North Mankato, Minnesota
052020
092020

THIS BOOK CONTAINS
RECYCLED MATERIALS

Design: Sarah DeYoung, Mighty Media, Inc.
Production: Mighty Media, Inc.
Editor: Liz Salzmann

Cover Photograph: Shutterstock Images
Interior Photographs: Aaron Vowels/Flickr, pp. 18, 19; David Stanley/Wikimedia Commons, pp. 7 (Fremantle), 27; Don Harrison/Flickr, p. 22; Dwight Burdette/Wikimedia Commons, pp. 6 (Eloise Psychiatric Hospital), 20–21; Nicolas Henderson/Flickr, pp. 6 (Yorktown), 25; Royasfoto73/Wikimedia Commons, pp. 7 (Waverly Hills), 17; Shutterstock Images, pp. 4–5, 6, 7, 10–11, 13, 28 (all), 29 (all); Tanya Moutzalias/AP Images, p. 23; Tim Kiser/ Wikimedia Commons, pp. 6 (Trans-Allegheny), 8–9; True British Metal/Flickr, pp. 7 (Poveglia), 15
Design Elements: Shutterstock Images

Library of Congress Control Number: 2020932464

Publisher's Cataloging-in-Publication Data
Names: Rusick, Jessica, author.
Title: Spooky hospitals / by Jessica Rusick
Description: Minneapolis, Minnesota : Abdo Publishing, 2021 | Series: Spooky spots | Includes online resources and index
Identifiers: ISBN 9781532193347 (lib. bdg.) | ISBN 9781098211981 (ebook)
Subjects: LCSH: Haunted places--Juvenile literature. | Ghosts--Juvenile literature. | Hospitals--Juvenile literature. | Spirits--Juvenile literature.
Classification: DDC 133.12--dc23

CONTENTS

HAUNTED HOSPITALS

Do you believe there are ghosts among us? Many people do. Whether you're a believer or not, old hospitals are some of the spookiest spots around!

Get ready to **explore** some of the most haunted hospitals on Earth. Walk through a maze of dark hallways. Shine a flashlight over peeling paint and rusted beds. But look out! You may not be alone.

Most hospitals thought to be haunted are no longer in use.

World's Spookiest
HOSPITALS

Are you ready for a ghostly adventure? Then pack up your wits and your **courage**. Let's take a trip to some of the world's spookiest hospitals!

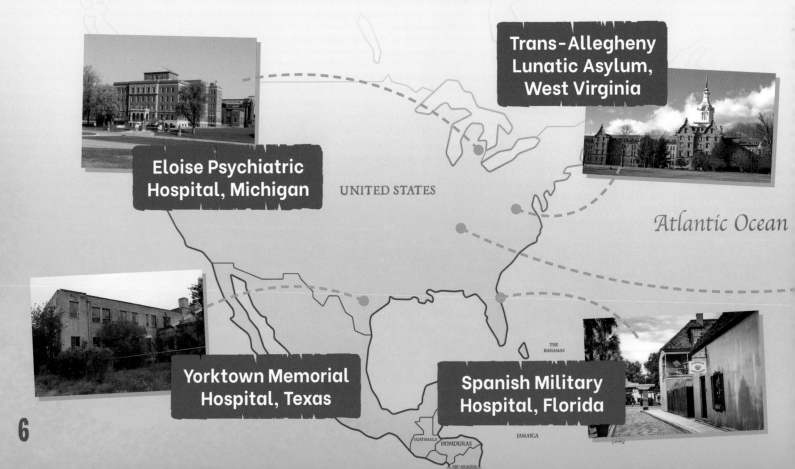

Trans-Allegheny Lunatic Asylum, West Virginia

Eloise Psychiatric Hospital, Michigan

UNITED STATES

Atlantic Ocean

Yorktown Memorial Hospital, Texas

Spanish Military Hospital, Florida

THE BAHAMAS

GUATEMALA
HONDURAS
JAMAICA
NICARAGUA

Poveglia Asylum, Italy

Fremantle Lunatic Asylum, Australia

Waverly Hills Sanatorium, Kentucky

TRANS-ALLEGHENY LUNATIC ASYLUM

The Trans-Allegheny **Lunatic Asylum** is in Weston, West Virginia. It opened in 1864. The asylum was dirty and crowded. **Patients** were put in cages or chained to walls if they misbehaved.

The asylum closed in 1994. It is now open to visitors. Some visitors claim to see the ghosts of its patients. One such patient is Jesse, who is said to whisper in guests' ears.

The Trans-Allegheny Lunatic Asylum was meant to house 250 patients. But by the 1950s, more than 2,400 patients lived there.

Another ghost is a nine-year-old girl named Lily. She was born and died in the **asylum**. Some people say she walks the halls in a white dress, giggling and playing music.

There are reports that other ghosts have thrown things at visitors! Some people have taken pictures of mysterious balls of light in the hospital. They believe these lights are proof of the ghosts.

SPANISH MILITARY HOSPITAL

The Spanish Military Hospital in St. Augustine, Florida, treated soldiers in the 1700s and 1800s. In 1821, construction workers discovered thousands of human bones beneath the hospital! It turned out that the hospital was built on a Native American burial ground.

Today, the building is a hospital museum. Some people believe spirits still wander its halls. Visitors report seeing ghostly **imprints** on hospital beds. Others have heard screams and seen objects move on their own.

Before the bones were discovered, workers said they felt the presence of spirits in the Spanish Military Hospital.

POVEGLIA ASYLUM

Poveglia **Asylum** is on the small Italian island of Poveglia. It opened in 1922. The **legend** is that a doctor there killed many **patients**. He did cruel experiments on them. The doctor later died after falling from the asylum's bell tower.

Poveglia Asylum closed in 1968. But some people believe that the ghosts of the doctor and his patients remain there. Though the bell tower is gone, people traveling near the island claim to hear it ring. Today, people are not allowed to visit the island.

From 1793 to 1814, Poveglia Island was used to keep people who were sick with the plague separate from others.

WAVERLY HILLS SANATORIUM

Waverly Hills **Sanatorium** sits high on a hill in Louisville, Kentucky. The hospital opened in 1910 to treat **patients** with **tuberculosis**. At the time, there was no medicine to treat the **disease**. So, it is likely that thousands of Waverly patients died.

Workers used a secret tunnel to move dead bodies out of the hospital. It was called the "body **chute**." **Legend** says the tunnel is haunted by the dead who traveled through it.

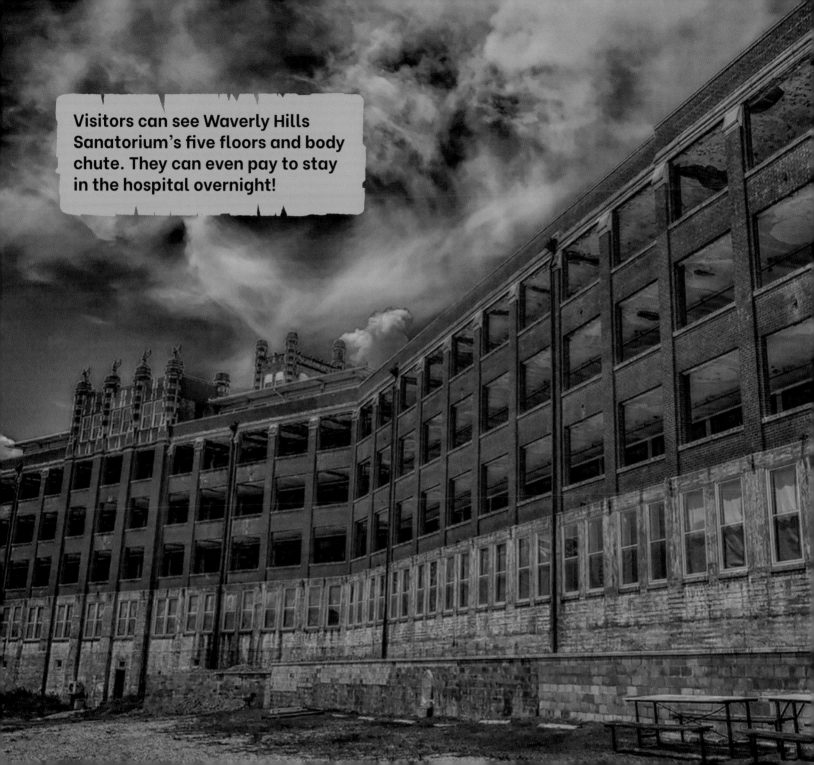

Visitors can see Waverly Hills Sanatorium's five floors and body chute. They can even pay to stay in the hospital overnight!

Today, Waverly Hills is open to the public. Visitors have reported seeing many scary sights. One is the Creeper. This shadowy, animallike figure is said to crawl up the hospital's walls and ceilings. People who see the Creeper report feeling sick and upset.

FRIGHTFUL FACT

Besides tours of the Waverly Hills Sanatorium, visitors can attend a haunted house there at Halloween.

Bodies were lowered down the 500-foot (152 m) chute using ropes and pulleys.

ELOISE PSYCHIATRIC HOSPITAL

The Eloise **Psychiatric** Hospital is in Westland, Michigan. It opened in 1839. The **patients** at Eloise lived in tiny rooms with bars on the windows.

Some patients even lived in a building that also housed pigs. People near the hospital could hear both patients crying and pigs squealing.

Eloise was once the largest psychiatric hospital in the United States, housing 10,000 patients.

The hospital closed in 1984. Today, visitors can tour the building. Many have reported hearing unexplained screams and moans. Some believe these noises come from the restless souls of former **patients**.

Visitors have also seen a woman in white wandering the upper floors. Some even claim to have found jars filled with human body parts!

FRIGHTFUL FACT

The Eloise Psychiatric Hospital was part of the Eloise Complex. This 900-acre (364 ha) area was like its own city. The Complex had its own fire station and train station.

The Eloise Complex also has a large graveyard. Instead of names, the gravestones simply have numbers. Most of the records of who is buried there are lost.

YORKTOWN MEMORIAL HOSPITAL

Yorktown Memorial Hospital is in the quiet town of Yorktown, Texas. The hospital was built in the 1950s. But it closed after 30 years. In that time, 2,000 **patients** had died.

Old furniture and medical tools were left behind. Visitors have reported seeing dark figures with glowing red eyes in the halls. Others have seen wheelchairs move on their own. Some visitors also claim there is a talking doll in the nursery. It asks, "Do you love me?"

One of the walls in Yorktown's basement is splattered with blood. Legend says two people were murdered there.

FREMANTLE LUNATIC ASYLUM

Fremantle **Lunatic Asylum** is in Australia. It opened in 1864. The asylum closed in 1900 after two **patients** died mysteriously. Today, the building is an arts center. But some people believe it is haunted by asylum patients.

Visitors have reported feeling someone touch or kiss them when no one is nearby. Others have reported hearing banging noises and feeling strange cold spots. And some claim to have heard a ghostly woman whisper, "Cold winds, that's what's in this place."

Patients at Fremantle were treated like prisoners. They had to shave their heads and wear prison uniforms.

SPOOKY OR SCIENCE?

You've just learned about some spooky hospitals. The creepy stories are fun! But good **explorers** look for reasons for what they see and hear. Strange happenings can often be explained by science.

Do you think the hospitals in this book are actually haunted? You might have to visit them to find out!

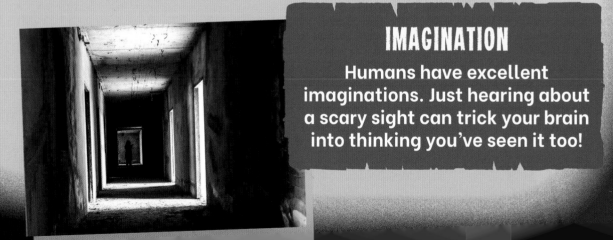

IMAGINATION

Humans have excellent imaginations. Just hearing about a scary sight can trick your brain into thinking you've seen it too!

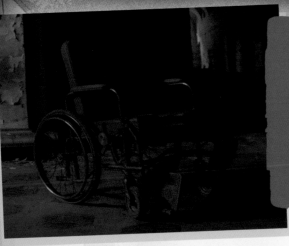

NATURAL PHENOMENON

Many old hospital buildings are drafty. At Yorktown Memorial Hospital, a puff of air could have caused the wheelchair to seem to roll on its own.

EXAGGERATION

Tourist sites may exaggerate spooky stories. They hope this will make more people want to visit.

SPOOKY PICTURES

Many visitors to haunted places report balls of light in their pictures. These are likely backscatter. Backscatter is when a camera's flash lights up specks of dust or water.

GLOSSARY

asylum – a place that protects and cares for people in need, especially people who are mentally ill.

chute – a tube or passage that people or things can slide down or drop through.

complex – a building or a group of buildings that are part of the same organization.

courage – strength or bravery.

disease – a sickness.

drafty – the condition of having a stream of cold air moving through a building or room.

exaggerate (ihg-ZA-juh-rayt) – to make something seem larger or more impressive.

explore – to go into in order to make a discovery or to have an adventure. A person who explores is an explorer.

imprint – a mark left on a surface by something that pressed against it.

legend – an old story that many people believe but cannot be proven true.

lunatic – an old-fashioned word for someone who is insane or mentally ill.

patient (PAY-shehnt) – a person who is under the care of a doctor.

psychiatric – relating to a type of medicine focusing on mental, emotional, or behavioral health.

sanatorium – a place for people who need a long time to recover from illness.

speck – a tiny dot or particle.

tourist site – a place people visit while on vacation.

tuberculosis – a serious sickness that affects the lungs.

ONLINE RESOURCES

Booklinks
NONFICTION NETWORK
FREE! ONLINE NONFICTION RESOURCES

To learn more about spooky hospitals, please visit **abdobooklinks.com** or scan this QR code. These links are routinely monitored and updated to provide the most current information available.

INDEX